AL CAPONE

A Dangerous Existence

BIOGRAPHY 7TH GRADE

Children's Biography Books

BABY PROFESSOR
EDUCATION KIDS

Speedy Publishing LLC
40 E. Main St. #1156
Newark, DE 19711
www.speedypublishing.com

In movies and stories, the greatest gangster in the U.S. in the early 20th century was Al Capone. Let's find out where he came from, what he did, and how his career ended.

A Gangster's Gangster

Al Capone was born in 1899, a child of an Italian immigrant family that moved to Brooklyn in 1894. Capone's father was an educated man who had worked as a barber. In New York they moved into a poor apartment in a tough area of Brooklyn, and became respectable members of the lively Italian community there.

Al Capone, around 1935.

Fritz Gordon, Al Capone and Mayor of Havana,
Julio Morales - Cuba.

Early Days

Capone started out in a loving family and a supportive community, even though it was a tough area. But he ran into bad, even terrible, situations in his early schooling that seem to have changed his character. He started out as a good student, but hit a woman teacher after an argument. He was expelled from school at age 14, and never continued his studies.

A Start In The Mob

Capone, at loose ends, met Johnny Torrio, a gangster. Torrio did not look like the kind of guy who would beat you up or steal your wallet, and he was the first of the new style of gang members. He taught Capone how important it was to have a respectable

front, and to let other people do your dirty work for you.

Mug shot of Italian-American mobster Johnny "Papa Johnny" Torrio.

NO. 397-CAL
TERMINAL ISLAND
1-7-39

However, it took a while for Capone to learn. He got involved in a fight in a bar as a young man, and had his face slashed. The prominent mark led to people calling him *"Scarface"*, a nickname he hated.

The day Al Capone arrived to the Federal Correctional Institution at Terminal Island in California, 1939.

Capone started in Torrio's gang. Torrio moved to Chicago in 1909 to run some mob operations there, and sent for Capone to work with him in 1920. This was the start of the Prohibition era, when alcohol

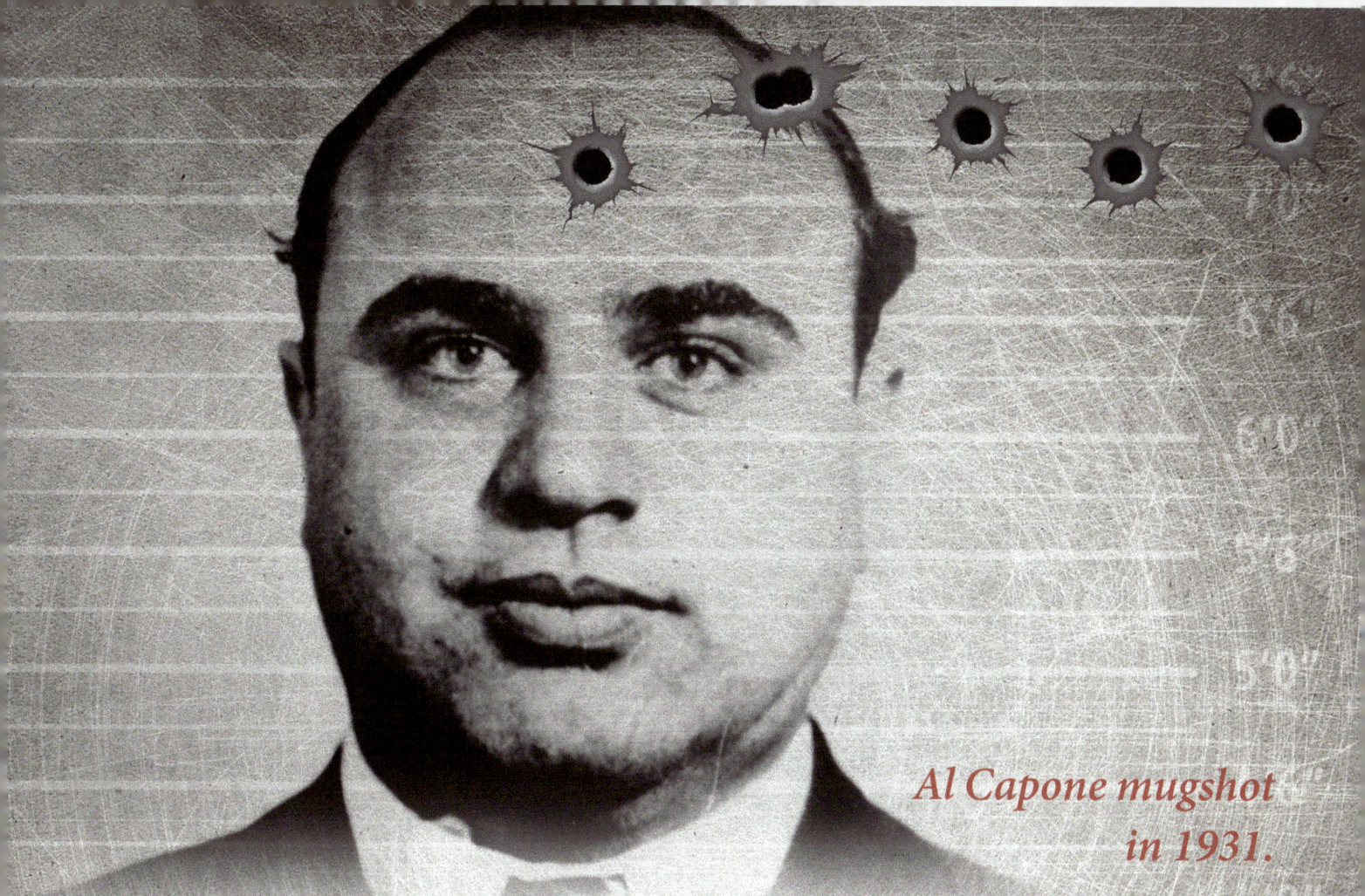

Al Capone mugshot in 1931.

was largely illegal in the United States, and gangs made enormous amounts of money by providing *"Bootleg"* alcohol to anyone who wanted it.

Al Capone's house at 7244 South Prairie Ave.
Chicago, Illinois.

Torrio retired in 1925, and Capone took over from him. This made him the top man in the organized crime network in Chicago. The gangs sold bootleg alcohol, managed illegal gambling operations, and offered other services that were illegal.

There were rival gangs in Chicago, and Capone maintained a steady war on them, having gang leaders, and even many gang members, assaulted or shot. He continued to absorb the operations of smaller gangs into his crime empire.

Frank 'The Enforcer' Nitti was a first cousin of Al Capone.

Keeping in mind Torrio's lessons, Capone presented himself as an innocent, law-abiding businessman. He never carried a gun...but he always had armed bodyguards with him.

Exteriors of Al Capone's house in Varadero, Cuba.

Gangster Jack McGurn

As the government of Chicago moved against criminal activities, Capone expanded his operations to the city of Cicero. Using bribes and blackmail, Capone's gang gained control of the city police department and politicians.

Louis Capone (left) and Emanuel "Mendy" Weiss (right),
American mobsters of the 1930s

Capone's older brothers, Frank and Ralph, took positions in the Cicero city government. Frank was shot and killed in a fight with the Chicago police force, but Al eventually got himself elected to office in Cicero.

Nucky Johnson and Al Capone.

The Crimes

Here are the sorts of things Al Capone's gang did:

· Election Tampering: Capone's people assaulted people working for other candidates and threatened voters to make them vote the *"right"* way.

- **Violence:** Although he normally left the rough stuff to others, when a friend got beaten up Capone found the man who had done it and shot him to death. No witnesses would come forward, although the murder happened in a crowded bar.

- **Violence Through Others:** To take over the bootleg whiskey business, Capone had members of a rival gang assaulted in what is called *"The Adonis Club Massacre"*.

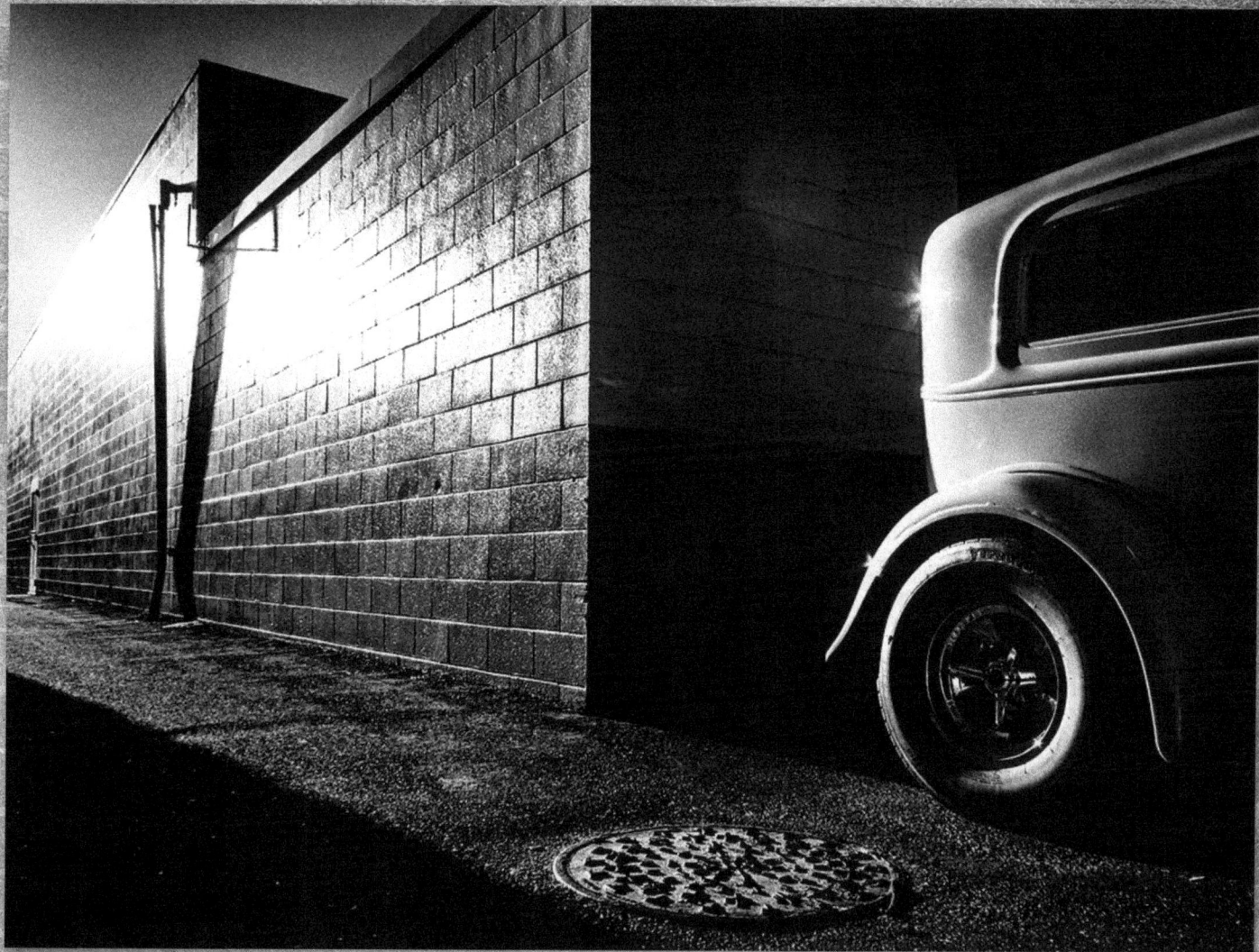

Vintage car parked in dark alley.

A police raid confiscating illegal alcohol.

·Illegal Activities: The gang made huge amounts of money by running gambling operations selling alcohol, both of which were illegal activities at the time. They used violence to defeat other gangs that wanted to do the same thing, and a combination of bribes and threats to keep politicians and the police away.

For a long while Capone had a very positive reputation as a powerful, but honest, man. But, in the course of a battle between Capone's gang and another group, a famous prosecutor named Billy McSwiggin was shot and killed. Capone was not charged with the crime, but his reputation suffered. As well, there was a rising outcry against organized crime in Chicago, making the

During the Great Depression unemployed men in line at a soup kitchen opened in Chicago by Al Capone The storefront sign reads 'Free Soup

police more bold and making it harder for the mob to continue its activities.

STREET VIOLENCE

Violence between different gangs in Chicago increased to the point that small armies were fighting each other in the streets, endangering not just themselves but anybody who happened to be nearby. One change for the worse was that the fighters started to use *"tommy guns"*, highly-

Legendary Machine-Gun Thomson

inaccurate machine guns that would throw a large number of bullets very quickly in the general direction of the target. Obviously, lots of people who were not the target ended up getting hit, and sometimes killed.

The St. Valentine's Day Massacre

An event that summed up what was going on in Chicago, and the way Capone dealt with his opponents, took place February 14, 1929.

One of Al Capone's rivals was Bugs Moran, who led a gang called the North Siders. Moran once tried to kill a friend of Capone's, so Capone set up a trap.

Saint Valentine's Day Massacre. Seven gangsters of Bugs Moran's gang were killed by Al Capone's in a garage in Chicago on Feb 14, 1929.

Portrait of a policeman

In the morning of February 14 Moran and his men were to go to a garage, supposedly to buy bootleg whiskey. Capone's men, dressed as policemen, would stage a *"raid"*.

Chicago gangster Bugs Moran.

The plan worked and Capone's men trapped and killed seven of the North Siders, shooting them with tommy guns. However, Moran had noticed one of the fake police cars nearby and got away before the shooting started.

A retro 1931 Ford car at the annual
Geneva Lake Classic Car Rally.

The slaughter became known as *"The St. Valentine's Day Massacre"*, and it was clear who had ordered the attack although Capone was never charged with it. People across the country now knew of Al Capone as a powerful, ruthless gang leader.

Comic book drawing of a gangster with a tommygun.

Tripped up

Al Capone worked carefully to make sure he could not be found guilty of any crime. However, he overlooked an angle that finally let law enforcement authorities catch him.

In 1927 the U.S. Supreme Court ruled that criminals had to pay income tax on the money they gained through illegal activities like gambling or bootlegging.

Sheriff dumps bootleg booze.

2'6"

Alfonso "Al" Capone Mansion in Miami, Florida.
The mansion was built in 1922.

The Special Intelligence Unit of the Internal Revenue Service started to build a case against Al Capone.

Capone tried to cover his tracks. He made almost all his purchases in cash, so there would be no record of what he spent. However, he had bought a huge estate in Florida and spent a lot renovating it. That flow of money had no honest explanation.

At the same time the U.S. Prohibition Bureau, which tried to stop bootlegging, began to put together a case on Capone and his gang. The head of this effort was Eliot Ness, and in dramatic movies he is the good guy who brings Capone down.

Eliot Ness

Photo of the cast for The Untouchables.

Capone was arrested in May, 1929 for carrying a concealed weapon. He stayed in jail until March, 1930. During this time government agents infiltrated the mob. This was a very dangerous job, and at least one agent was discovered and killed. However, the agents were able to put together evidence, and even secured two bookkeepers who knew all about the way the gang handled its money.

At the same time Eliot Ness directed raids on the gang's bootlegging operations, seizing millions of dollars' worth of equipment and destroying thousands of gallons of illegal

Orange County Sheriff's deputies dumping illegal booze, Santa Ana, 3-31-1932.

alcohol. They also managed to completely shut down the largest breweries the gang had used.

In March, 1931, the government charged Al Capone with tax evasion, claiming he owed over $32,000 in taxes on the money he made from criminal activity. A grand jury later charged him with 22 counts of tax evasion, which would have a penalty over $200,000.

"Scarface" Al Capone is shown here at the Chicago Detective bureau following his arrest.

The trial began in October, 1931. Capone's people had tried to bribe the jury, but the judge had set up a second, secret jury and used that jury in the trial. Capone's lawyer tried to show him as a sort of Robin-Hood character, stealing from the rich to give to the poor, but the prosecution showed details of Capone's lavish lifestyle as well as details of his cruel actions. On October 17,

Capone was found guilty of tax evasion. He was sentenced to jail for eleven years, with over $80,000 in fines.

Al Capone's Department of Justice, Bureau of Investigation arrest and criminal history record.

FINAL DAYS

Alcatraz "The Rock" was developed with facilities for a lighthouse, a military fortification, a military prison (1868), and a federal prison from 1933 until 1963.

Al Capone started serving his sentence in a prison in Atlanta. He and his gang were able to stay in close contact, and bribes of prison officials made his jail cell quite comfortable.

But in 1934 the authorities moved Capone to Alcatraz Prison, on an island off San Francisco. There were fewer privileges and much less contact with the outside world. In this period, Capone lost control of his gang.

Historic Prison Cell of Al Capone in Philadelpha's Eastern State Prison.

Capone's health was starting to go down hill, and he was often confused. After six and a half years in jail, he was released. He returned to his mansion in Florida and lived quietly there. He was consistently ill and confused in his mind. He finally died in early 1947 of a heart attack, at the age of 48.

Workmen at Mt. Olivet Cemetery in Chicago moving the vault with Al Capone's body. Feb. 6, 1947.

Choices

Al Capone chose to be a gangster, a murderer and a criminal. Nobody made him do these things. Read about young men who made very different choices in the Baby Professor books *A Rich Man in Poor Clothes: The Story of St. Francis of Assisi* and *Marquis de Lafayette: The Hero of Two Worlds*.

Al Capone at the Madame Tussauds museum in SF.

Visit

BABY PROFESSOR
EDUCATION KIDS

www.BabyProfessorBooks.com

to download Free Baby Professor eBooks
and view our catalog of new and exciting
Children's Books

9 798869 413529